Thanks for
helping with
Sunday School
this year!

In Christ,
Cara

Look Through
God-Colored Glasses

Look Through God-Colored Glasses
Copyright © 2009 by Zondervan

Requests for information should be addressed to:
Zondervan, *Grand Rapids, Michigan 49530*

ISBN 978-0-310-31847-7

Interior Design by Melissa Elenbaas

Printed in China

_____

09 10 11 12 • 5 4 3 2 1

Content in this book excerpted from
God Is Closer Than You Think by John Ortberg.

God Is Everywhere

God is closer than we think. He is never farther than a prayer away. All it takes is the barest effort, the lift of a finger. Every moment—this moment right now, as you read these words—is the "one timeless moment" of divine endowment, of life with God.

God talks through burning bushes and braying donkeys; he sends messages through storms and rainbows and earthquakes and dreams, he whispers in a still small voice. He speaks (in the words of Garrison Keillor) in "ordinary things like cooking and small talk, through storytelling ,making love, fishing, tending animals and sweet corn and flowers, through sports, music, and books, raising kids—all the places where the gravy soaks in and grace shines through."

The story of the Bible isn't primarily about the desire of people to be with God; it's the desire of God to be with people.

One day I was sitting on a plane next to a businessman. The screen saver on his computer was the picture of a towheaded little boy taking what looked like his first shaky step. "Is that your son?" I asked.

Yes, that was the man's son, his only child. Let's say his name was Adam. The man told me about his son's first step and first word with a sense of wonder, as if Adam had invented locomotion and speech. He had a whole string of pictures of Adam doing things that pretty much all children do, and he displayed them one at a time.

Why was the man so preoccupied with Adam? Because he looked at him through the eyes of a father. Everything Adam did was cloaked with wonder. It didn't matter that other children do them as well.

And then it hit me. I am the child on God's screen saver. And so are you. The tiniest details of our lives never grow old to him. God himself is filled with wonder at our faltering steps and stammering words—not because we do them better than anyone else, but because he views them through the eyes of a loving Father. God shows our pictures to the angels until even the angels get a little tired of looking.

The central promise in the Bible is not "I will forgive you," although of course that promise is there. It is not the promise of life after death, although we are offered that as well. The most frequent promise in the Bible is "I will be *with* you."

"Find a place in your heart," said an ancient sage named Theophan the Recluse, "and speak there with the Lord. It is the Lord's reception room." Some people seem to find this room easily.

Some people seem to have a kind of inner radar for detecting the presence of God. Just as certain musicians have perfect pitch, these people have an ear for discerning God's voice. They seem to be as aware of God as they are of gravity. Telling them how to look for God would be like telling a fish how to look for water—where else could they live?

I believe my life hinges on the presence of God. I know that courage and guidance and hope all reside with him. But I am aware of the gap—even if it is only a hairbreadth. And in the midst of all my ambiguity—my weakness and occasional spiritual indifference—I long for the touch that will close the gap.

Consider Michelangelo Buonar-
roti's brilliant painting of God and Adam on the
ceiling of the Sistine Chapel. If you look carefully
at the painting, you notice that the finger of God is
extended toward the man with great vigor.

This is the story of the God of the Sistine Chapel. God is still in the business of coming down to earth: to this cubicle, this email, this room, this house, this job, this hospital room, this car, this bed, this vacation. Any place can become Bethel, the house of God. Cleveland, maybe. Or the chair you're sitting in as you read these words.

Once you see God in an ordinary moment at an ordinary place, you never know where he'll show up next. You could start seeing him anywhere— even in the face of someone who's been your mortal enemy for twenty years.

God is closer than you think.

Set aside for now the question of to what extent any of us is capable of experiencing God's presence in our current spiritual condition.

The teaching of scripture is that God really is present right here, right now. Michelangelo's picture really does express spiritual reality. The Spirit of God is available to you and me: flowing all the time, welling up within us, quenching our unsatisfied desires, overflowing to refresh those around us. He is at work all the time, in every place. And every once in a while somebody somewhere wakes up.

Spiritual growth, in a sense, is simply increasing our capacity to experience the presence of God.

Maybe I miss God because I fail to see him in the ordinary moments of my life. Maybe every heartbeat is not just the mechanism of a sophisticated plumbing system but the echo of God's voice, the murmur of God's love. There are people—saints and mystics—who seem to find God in their lives as easily as the morning newspaper. They check their hearts and feel him walking around in there.

God is always present and active in my life, whether or not I see him.

Coming to recognize and experience God's presence is *learned* behavior; I can cultivate it.

My task is to meet God in *this* moment.

Waldo And
Rainbow Days

On Michelangelo's ceiling, all Adam has to do is lift a finger and he can touch the hand of God. God is that close.

But sometimes I wish God would show himself more plainly, maybe come down from the clouds every once in a while and part Lake Michigan so I could see for myself. He is, after all, invisible, inaudible, and untouchable.

Waldo will never make it to the Sistine Chapel. Waldo is a geeky-looking, glasses-wearing nerd with a striped shirt and goofy hat created by an illustrator named Martin Handford who wanted to draw crowd scenes.

This guy Waldo is supposed to be on every page. The author assures us that it is so. But you couldn't prove it by me. He is often hidden to the untrained eye. You have to be willing to look for him. Children grew fascinated with trying to find their hero—so fascinated that more than 40 million "Where's Waldo" books have been sold in twenty-eight countries.

When you find Waldo there is a sense of joy and accomplishment. In fact, developing the capacity to track him down is part of the point of the book.

But sometimes it takes a while to find Waldo. It demands patience. Some people are better at it than others. Some people just give up.

Part of what makes it hard to find Waldo is that he is so ordinary-looking. In the initial pages his presence is obvious. Later on, he's hidden.

Like Waldo, let every day, every moment, of your life be another page. God is there, the Scriptures tell us—on every one of them. But the ease with which he may be found varies from one page to the next.

LOOK THROUGH GOD-COLORED GLASSES

When each of my three children was born, I was seized by the conviction that something more than just a blob of tissue had entered the world. I knew I had been invited to witness the supernatural. When I watched my children enter the world, I could not not believe. It was as if God himself were in the room. (Which may be why my wife said his name a lot during labor.) The births of my children were rainbow days.

On rainbow days your life is filled with too much goodness and meaning for you to believe it is simply by chance. On rainbow days you find yourself wanting to pray, believing that God hears, open to receiving and acting on his response. On rainbow days God seems to speak personally to you through Scripture.

It can be easy to take rainbow days for granted or assume they will go on forever. But that's a big mistake.

People who are wise learn to treasure rainbow days as gifts. They store them up to remember on days when God seems more elusive. One of the dangers in this, however, is that we may start to think we have earned them, that they are a reflection of our spiritual maturity.

Why doesn't God make every day a rainbow day and send epiphanies twenty-four-seven? Maybe it's because God wants us to learn to see him in the ordinary rather than be dependent on the extraordinary. Maybe it's because if God regularly satisfied our demand for special effects it would be like a mother who inadvertently trains her children to pay attention only when she raises her voice.

Psychologists who deal with the study of perception refer to a phenomenon called "habituation." The idea is that when a new object of stimulus is introduced to our environment, we are intensely aware of it, but the awareness fades over time. So, for instance, when we first begin to wear a new wrist watch, we feel it on our wrist constantly, but after a while we don't even notice that it's there.

Years ago we had a dog that used to eat our furniture. When I say "eat," I don't mean "chew on." He ate the top off the ottoman in front of our sofa so that the foam rubber was exposed, then he ate most of the foam rubber. The pathetic part is, we got used to a half-eaten, foam-rubber-exposed ottoman. After a while we didn't even notice it anymore. We habituated.

One of the greatest challenges in life is fighting what might be called spiritual habituation. We simply drift into acceptance of life in spiritual maintenance mode.

When life is on spiritual autopilot,

— I yell at my children.

— I worry too much about money or my job.

— I get jealous of people more successful or attractive than I.

— I use deception to get out of trouble.

— I pass judgment on people, often when I am secretly jealous of them.

Spiritual habituation is in some ways more dangerous than spiritual depravity because it can be so subtle, so gradual. Mostly it involves a failure to see.

Nancy and I have discovered a strange parenting phenomenon. When we raise the volume level to get our children's attention, they pretty quickly tune us out. But when we lower our voices to speak about something private with each other (birthday present, maybe, or modes of punishment), our kids become instantly attentive. Words we try to whisper will be heard three rooms and two closed doors away. It is as if our children have an inner instinct for when we are trying to keep information from them and suddenly develop auditory abilities that CIA operatives would pay for.

Maybe the reason God lowers his voice is so we will learn to pay attention.

A cinematographer, Bob Fisher, wrote a passionate article recently about the need for movie crews to spend some time very day reviewing the film that was shot the day before. By delaying production temporarily to review the previous day's work, filmmakers can spot little mistakes while they can still be corrected and can celebrate what is going right. In Fisher's words, "Watching film dailies is uplifting. It energizes everyone."

In a similar way, it's a very helpful thing for us to take a few moments to "review the dailies" with God. You can do this right now by walking through yesterday in your mind with God and asking where he was present and at work in each scene. Start with the moment when you woke up in the morning. God was present, waking you up, giving you a mini-resurrection. What were your first thoughts? What do you think God wanted to say to you in that moment?

Go on from one scene to the next through your day. As I review what happened when I greeted my family, ate breakfast, and went through meetings at work, I see patterns emerging—the ongoing presence of anxiety or anger—that I miss when I don't take time to review the dailies. Most of all, I look and listen to see how God is speaking to me through these scenes. I realize he was talking to me through the words of another person or the lines of a book or the therapy of laughter. The more often I review, the better I get at recognizing him in "real time."

But sometimes it seems that God cannot be found even though we really want to find him. Perhaps in his hiddenness, God is up to something.

God wants to be known, but not in a way that overwhelms us, that takes away the possibility of love freely chosen. "God is like a person who clears his throat while hiding and so gives himself away," said Meister Eckhart.

LOOK THROUGH GOD-COLORED GLASSES

Where's God? He's right around the corner. He's lurking where you least expect him. He's right there on the page. He's anywhere people are willing to see the whole world with eyes incapable of anything but wonder, and with a tongue fluent only in praise.

Define The
Relationship

D.T.R. —You most likely know what this is if you're under thirty. The letters stand for "Define the Relationship." It generally gets used in relationships between a man and a woman that have romantic overtones but are squishy about permanence and exclusivity. It is a clarion call for relational clarity: Are we in this relationship for laughs, or are we in it for keeps?

To "sit at someone's feet" was a technical expression in ancient times to indicate the relationship between a disciple and a rabbi. To make someone your rabbi was fundamentally a choice about being with him. A disciple was someone who had chosen to be with his rabbi as much as possible in order to learn everything he could from him.

So what keeps us from being covered with the dust of the rabbi? What keeps us from living in the presence of God? Ironically, it is usually not that we have deliberately chosen to keep him at arm's length. It is something much more insidious and subtle.

We have good intentions, but we end up missing out on God's presence—not because we've rejected him, but because we just get overwhelmed by preparations for life. We get distracted. We forget to look for Waldo on the page. Same house, different rooms, and the primary indicator is worry.

I took my daughters to see the movie Snow White when they were quite young. I realized partway through the movie—this is a horrible model for them.

Here's a woman who—

- Hides from her stepmother because she feels worried and upset;

- Takes a job doing menial labor for seven short, cranky guys, because she thinks she could never find more fulfilling work;

- Sits around passively waiting to get rescued, singing "Some day my prince will come. . ."

I wanted my little girls to know that if you're ever in that situation—

- Confront your stepmother face-to-face. Tell her to come to grips with the aging process and you have no intention of being the fall guy because of her neurotic insecurities about facing sexual attractiveness, so it's time for her to find a good therapist.

- Tell the seven short guys to get a life. If they can't handle basic challenges of personal hygiene and housekeeping, they'll have to find some other codependent to enable their domestic passivity.

- Stop waiting for some prince to come around and rescue you. Build deep relationships, find meaningful work, serve the poor, deepen your mind.

And when it is time to choose a prince—let Daddy decide who the prince should be.

Your Greatest Moment

Now can be the greatest moment of your life because this moment is the place where you can meet God. In fact, this moment is the *only* place where you can meet God.

This is why one of the greatest books of spiritual advice ever written was given the inspired title *The Sacrament of the Present Moment.*

If this is the greatest moment of life, I want to suggest what might be the single most dangerous word in the English language—*tomorrow*. *Let's wait until tomorrow.*

People persistently tolerate and maintain behavioral patterns that will destroy their own lives. *Tomorrow* may cause us to mismanage finances; it may mean constant problems at work; it can damage relationships; it can eat up our self-esteem and erode our joy. But none of these scenarios gets to the root of the problem.

What matters most is this: God is present in this instant, offering to partner with us in whatever we face. The failure to embrace the "sacrament of the present moment" will keep us from being fully present to God right here, right now.

We think the great adventure of partnership with God lies somewhere in the future. Some people go through their whole life in that frame of mind.

"God is closer than you think" means he is available in *this moment right now*. Always now. Only now.

Spending the day with God does not usually involve doing different things from what we already do. Mostly it involves learning to do what we already do in a new way—*with God.*

In Jewish life, the Sabbath begins not at sunup but at sundown. In this way the biblical writers help us to remember: Everything doesn't depend on me. I go to sleep, God goes to work. It's his day. The world keeps spinning, tides ebb and flow, lives begin and end even though I am not there to superintend any of it. God is present when I sleep.

LOOK THROUGH GOD-COLORED GLASSES

How do you wake up *with God?* This may be very hard for you. There are two kinds of people: those who love to get up in the morning, and those who hate those who love to get up in the morning. You may be in the second camp.

Instead of forcing yourself in the morning, try to arrange—as early as you can after you wake up—to have just a few minutes alone with God. Do three things:

- Acknowledge your dependence on God. *I won't live through this day banking on my own strength and power.*

- Tell God about your concerns for the day, and ask him to identify and remove any fear in you. I often do this with my calendar for the day open before me.

Renew your invitation for God to spend the day with you.

Something as mundane as washing up in the morning is something we can do with God. In ancient times, cleansing and purification were a very important and highly symbolic part of life. Priests had to go through a very elaborate process of cleansing before entering the temple. This served as a kind of reminder of the need for our souls to be cleansed.

Food too, is a gift from God. To the writers of Scripture, food is concrete evidence that God is present and providing.

If you think trying to turn eating into a spiritual experience is a little far-fetched, consider that for the ancient Hebrews, the other end of the digestive process was a gift of God as well. They actually had a prayer to be said after going to the bathroom: "Blessed art Thou, O God, who has made the openings in my body."

Nothing can separate us from the love of God.

It can be helpful to keep certain physical reminders of God's presence nearby. I have some stones with certain words inscribed on them that speak deeply to me about God's care. One stone reads "Joy." Another says "Courage." A third one just has the word "Yes." Each reminds me of the spirit in which I want to work. They tell me that I'm not alone.

At the end of my workday I used to become discouraged at what I didn't accomplish. Now I try to do what God did during the week of creation: to look at what has been accomplished that day and celebrate what is good. I thank God that he has partnered with me through the day. I take a moment to ask him to partner with me tomorrow.

Open Your Mind To God

LOOK THROUGH GOD-COLORED GLASSES

Two people live with meager financial resources. One of them is consumed by envy and discontent; the other is radiant with gratitude and servanthood. Their net worth is the same. The difference is in their minds.

The mind is an instrument of staggering potential. But its potential is not measured by IQ or academic degrees. For it is in our minds that we live in conscious awareness of and interaction with God.

Throughout history, those who have practiced God's presence most have insisted that they hear his voice. They have learned, so to speak, to program their minds to be constantly receiving the divine channel. "The word is very near you; it is in your mouth and in your heart so you may obey it."

If we are going to be in a personal relationship with someone, there must be some two-way communication. Even the most uncommunicative husband has to grunt every once in a while or it isn't a marriage—it's a monologue. The God of the Bible is not limited to grunting.

So being *with* God is something that takes place primarily in our thoughts, our mind.

God is infinite rather than finite, so he is able to guide our thoughts directly. He can speak to us through Scripture, of course, or through the words of another person. But he also has "direct access," so to speak; he can plant a thought directly in our minds. Anytime. Anywhere.

We cannot force God's speaking, and it is not wise to try. But there are things we can do to make our minds increasingly receptive to his presence in our thoughts.

In the painting on the ceiling of the Sistine Chapel, God and the man he created are just a hairbreadth apart. How far apart is that? Closer than you think. *God is never more than a single thought away.* Even if I haven't thought of him for days. Even when I have been immersed in selfishness and sin.

The reality is that your mind is never still. You are having thoughts, observations, perceptions, and ideas at such a staggering rate that you don't even remember the vast majority of them.

In time, if we listen carefully, we can learn to recognize God's voice. Not infallibly, of course. But the kind of thoughts that come from God are those in line with the fruit of the Spirit; they move us toward love and joy and peace and patience.

Our job is to be ruthless about saying yes when we believe God is speaking to us. Every time we do, we will get a little more sensitive to hearing him the next time. Our mind becomes a little more receptive, a little more tuned in to God's channel. On the other hand, when we say, "No, I'd rather stay in my aisle seat," we make ourselves a little less likely to hear him in the future.

Only God can change a mind. When God is present in a mind, it begins to flow with a new kind of thought.

Make your mind the dwelling place of God. The goal is to have a mind in which the glorious Father is always present and gradually crowds out every distorted belief, every destructive feeling, every misguided intention. You will know your mind is increasingly "set on God" when the moods that dominate your inner life are love, joy, and peace—the three primary components of the fruit of the Spirit.

We often want to be able to hear guidance from God about important decisions such as whom to marry or what job to take. But we also want to reserve the right to feed our minds on whatever junk comes along. Ultimately this makes our minds receptive or deaf toward the still small voice of God.

Often God uses other people to help us discern his voice. There are certain people in your life whose words consistently guide you toward truth and joy and love. Be sure you make time for those people.

Pathways To God

All too often we fail to realize that our individual uniqueness means we will all experience God's presence and learn to relate to him in different ways, in ways that correspond to the wiring patterns he himself created in us.

God wants to be fully present with each of us. But because he made us to be different from one another, we are not identical in the activities and practices that will help us connect with him.

A spiritual pathway has to do with the way we most naturally sense God's presence and experience spiritual growth.

There is enormous freedom in identifying and embracing your spiritual pathway. It is a little like realizing that if you're an introvert you don't *have* to work as a salesman; you could get a job in a library.

People on an intellectual pathway draw closer to God as they learn more about him.

People who follow the relational pathway find that they have a deep sense of God's presence when they're involved in significant relationships.

On the serving pathway people find that God's presence seems most tangible when they are involved in helping others.

For people on the worship pathway, something deep inside them feels released when praise and adoration are given voice.

If you have an activist pathway, you have a high level of energy. You are a zeal junkie.

If you have a contemplative pathway, you love large blocks of uninterrupted time alone.

Creation types find that they have a passionate ability to connect with God when they are experiencing the world he made.

Once we know which pathways are ours, how do we use this information to help us experience God's closeness? We need to accept and embrace the unique way God created us. Instead of following "mass production" approaches to spiritual growth, we need to make sure that we spend adequate time and activity pursuing the pathways that most help us connect with God.

Believing Is Seeing

At the borderline of our yard is a hedge. It is growing over a fence, so we cannot see or pass through to the other side. It has become an obsession for Winston, our Yorkshire terrier. Winston is on constant patrol duty. He is sensitive to every creature that goes through our property. He hears sounds and smells scents that are undetectable to the rest of us. And Winston is convinced that there is Something on the other side of the hedge.

We don't know what it is. Maybe it's just rabbits and squirrels. Maybe it's a giant, silent mastiff. Maybe it's a beautiful girl-dog pumping out canine Love Potion #9.

The hedge is a veil, a barrier that traps me in the aloneness of my backyard and cuts me off from some larger Presence. The hedge keeps me from seeing. The hedge is my finitude, my loneness, my blindness, my sin.

Every day, millions of times a day, a heart stops beating, a pair of lungs stops breathing, and the hedge ceases to be their reality. If anyone could figure out a way to come back and give us a description of the other side, they could make a nice living. Some folks say they have gotten close enough to see a bright light, but they can offer no details. Others, like actress Shirley MacLaine, have claimed to go back and forth on a regular basis.

Some people are convinced that there is Nothing behind the hedge, that our backyard is all there is, that what you see is what you get. But the whispers and rumors of the Presence are curiously stubborn. There seems to be in the human race an irrepressible instinct that Something lies behind the hedge, that there is more to existence than a swirl of molecules and atoms, that death is a gate and not a fence, that reality is bigger than just our backyard.

Those who believe that Something lies behind the hedge must struggle with why the hedge is there at all. Why does the Something stay so hidden? Does the hedge serve a purpose? Is it possible that there is some good in not knowing?

Those who believe that Nothing lies behind the hedge must struggle with why the rumors of Something are so persistent. Harder still, they must struggle with what to do during our brief time in the backyard if the backyard turns out to be nothing more than a cemetery.

Sometimes people pray a version of the *Star Trek* prayer to Scottie: "Beam me up." Many people think our job is to get my afterlife destination taken care of, then tread water till we all get ejected and God comes back and torches this place.

God doesn't reveal himself to us just to make us happy or to deliver us from loneliness. He also comes to us so that we can in turn be conduits of his presence to other people. He invites us to join him in making things down here the way they are up there.

Start by asking yourself this question: "Where do I want to see God's presence and power break into my world? Where would I especially like God to use me to make things down here run the way they do up there?"

One day a little beachhead got formed in your life. It doesn't matter whether your life seems messy to you. It doesn't matter if you don't fully understand how the kingdom works. Someone has come from the other side of the hedge. And he uses you and me. He lives in our backyard now.

Text in this title was excerpted from *God Is Closer Than You Think* by John Ortberg. This title is available at your local bookstore.

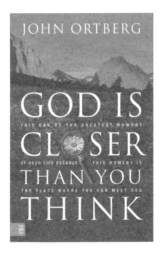

978-0-310-25349-5